CELEBRATING THE CITY OF AGRA

Celebrating the City of Agra

Walter the Educator

Silent King Books

SILENT KING BOOKS

SKB

Copyright © 2024 by Walter the Educator

All rights reserved. No part of this book may be reproduced in any manner whatsoever without written permission except in the case of brief quotations embodied in critical articles and reviews.

First Printing, 2024

Disclaimer
This book is a literary work; the story is not about specific persons, locations, situations, and/or circumstances unless mentioned in a historical context. Any resemblance to real persons, locations, situations, and/or circumstances is coincidental. This book is for entertainment and informational purposes only. The author and publisher offer this information without warranties expressed or implied. No matter the grounds, neither the author nor the publisher will be accountable for any losses, injuries, or other damages caused by the reader's use of this book. The use of this book acknowledges an understanding and acceptance of this disclaimer.

Celebrating the City of Agra is a little collectible souvenir book that belongs to the Celebrating Cities Book Series by Walter the Educator. Collect them all and more books at WaltertheEducator.com

USE THE EXTRA SPACE TO TAKE NOTES AND DOCUMENT YOUR MEMORIES

AGRA

Beneath the golden Indian sun,

Celebrating the City of
Agra

Where rivers of history eternally run,

Lies Agra, a city of timeless grace,

A jewel, a legend, a storied place.

Whispers of empires in the wind,

Eternal tales that never rescind,

Echoes of Mughal glory stand,

In the heart of this ancient land.

Agra, where the Yamuna flows,

A river of dreams, where history glows,

Reflecting palaces, gardens, and skies,

Celebrating the City of
Agra

Where the past and present harmonize.

Through bustling bazaars, a vibrant spree,

Of colors and scents, a sensory sea,

Where spices and silks in rhythm align,

A mosaic of culture, rich and divine.

The Taj Mahal, an ethereal sight,

A marble marvel in the moonlight,

Its domes and minarets kiss the skies,

A testament to love that never dies.

Shah Jahan's dream, Mumtaz's tomb,

Celebrating the City of
Agra

A love story that eternally blooms,

In Agra's heart, their spirits reside,

In the whispers of the Yamuna's tide.

The Red Fort stands, a sentinel old,

With walls of sandstone, stories untold,

Within its ramparts, echoes of the past,

Mughal splendor, forever to last.

Jahangir's palace, Akbar's throne,

In every stone, a history known,

A fusion of cultures, a grand display,

Of Persian artistry and Indian sway.

Fatehpur Sikri, a city of dreams,

Where Akbar's vision eternally gleams,

Red sandstone structures, silent yet proud,

A whispering city, a memory loud.

to Agra, proud and grand,

A gem that sparkles in this land,

A place where history and love entwine,

In the heart of Agra, forever shine.

Celebrating the City of
Agra

ABOUT THE CREATOR

Walter the Educator is one of the pseudonyms for Walter Anderson. Formally educated in Chemistry, Business, and Education, he is an educator, an author, a diverse entrepreneur, and he is the son of a disabled war veteran. "Walter the Educator" shares his time between educating and creating. He holds interests and owns several creative projects that entertain, enlighten, enhance, and educate, hoping to inspire and motivate you.

Follow, find new works, and stay up to date with Walter the Educator™ at WaltertheEducator.com

www.ingramcontent.com/pod-product-compliance
Lightning Source LLC
LaVergne TN
LVHW052007060526
838201LV00059B/3892